The Temptations of Jesus
His Victory and Ours

ISBN: 0-8341-0871-2

10 9 8 7 6 5 4 3 2 1

Cover design: Royce Ratcliff

Illustration: The Temptation of Christ, ca. 1535, by
                 Tiziano Vecelli (called Titian); The
                 Minneapolis Institute of Arts.

Dedication

These talks were given to a group of professional youth ministers from several denominations in retreat at Glen Eyrie, Colorado.

Youth ministers serve in a unique context. They live with their own visions; they live among the young in their own youth culture; yet they serve in the traditional structure and expectation of the church. I have been a college chaplain; I think I understand them.

And so does our Lord. His temptations reveal His own struggles of self-understanding and ministry in the face of human need and religious expectation and social structure. He won the victory through His temptations, and His victory is one we may share. That is the point of this book.

I gratefully dedicate it to the youth ministers of that Glen Eyrie retreat and to their peers who know the special temptations and the special victories of ministry among the young.

—REUBEN WELCH
San Diego

The Temptations
of Jesus:
His Victory
and Ours

by

Reuben Welch

Beacon Hill Press of Kansas City
Kansas City, Missouri

Contents

*Then Jesus came from Galilee to the Jordan
to John, to be baptized by him. . . . And when
Jesus was baptized, he went up immediately
from the water, and behold, the heavens were
opened and he saw the Spirit of God
descending like a dove, and alighting on him;
and lo, a voice from heaven, saying, "This is
my beloved Son, with whom I am well
pleased."*
Matt. 3:13, 16-17

1

Am I Who the Father
Says I Am?

I think the baptism and the temptation of Jesus
are two fascinating things to think about.
I've often thought about how Jesus must have felt
when the rumors reached Galilee from
down in Judea by the Dead Sea,
there at the Jordan River
where John was baptizing.
I've wondered what feelings were inside Him.
Through all those years in the carpenter shop,
as far as we know, He hadn't said anything
profound
or done anything special.

But when the word came
that John was in the wilderness
baptizing,
something stirred in His inner heart;
and He hung His
carpenter's tools
on the pegs of the wall
for the last time.
How did it feel
to hang those tools on those pegs
and walk away?
Something was going on inside Him.
Something had been going on inside Him for a long
time.
One of the fun things we do in the classes I teach
is talk about the unanswerable questions.
*Don't you like to talk about
the unanswerable questions—
and then everybody's right!*

One of those questions is:
When was it that Jesus came to full knowledge of who
He was?
Have you ever thought about that?
At what point in His life did Jesus understand Himself
to be the
Son of God?
I'm sure we know that He had no real self-
consciousness
as a babe in a manger.
We know, don't we, that Jesus,
as He was cradled in His mother's arms,
was *not* saying to himself,
"Oh, so this is what it feels like
to be a baby"?

10

I hope you don't believe that.
I hope you believe that He was a real,
live, growing person.
And somewhere in His growing years something
began to happen.
Alongside His ordinary human development,
a sense of unique identity was emerging.
Luke's snapshot of the Temple episode when He
was twelve
gives us a little glimpse of those beginnings.
After three days,
His mother said,
Your father and I have been
looking for you anxiously.
And Jesus said,
Did you not know that I must be
in my Father's house? (Luke 2:48-49)
The word *father* had two different meanings.
His mother said, "Your *father* and I."
But Jesus said, "My *Father's* house."
There was some new sense of
relationship
some new openness to His Father
and new awareness of who He was.

But it's hard for me to believe that a 12-year-old
has a complete sense of self-identity.
Maybe more than I think.
At any rate, Luke says that after this event
He went home with His parents,
was subject to them,
and **increased in wisdom**
and in stature,
and in favor with God and man. (Luke 2:52)
And whatever insight came to Jesus
in the Temple at that time,

it was partial
it was youthful
and it was followed by a
long period
of growth and development.

And I think
that in those growing years
there was developing inside Him an
ever-deepening awareness of himself as the
Son of God.
But it didn't show, and nothing occurred during His
early years
to lead anyone around Him
to expect anything significant from Him.
He led a very common
ordinary
growing life.

I believe that.

Remember when He went back to Nazareth,
back to the synagogue where He had been
brought up?
He opened the scroll and read out of Isaiah:
The Spirit of the Lord is upon me,
because he has anointed me
to preach
good news ... proclaim release
to the captives ...
proclaim the acceptable
year of the Lord.
(Luke 4:18-19)
And He closed the book and said,
Today this scripture has been
fulfilled in your hearing.
(Luke 4:21)

They all heard the gracious words
that proceeded out of His mouth.
And then, as they were in dialogue with one another,
they said,
   Isn't this Joseph's son?
   Don't we know His brothers and sisters?
    Aren't they here among us?
    Who is this?
    Where does He get all this stuff?
        And they were offended
      by Him.
     And the story ends
     with their taking Him out
    to push Him over the brow of
    the hill.
   But He passed through the crowd
      and went His way.
Evidently, nothing in His growing years had led
 His peers
to expect anything special from Him.
  When it came, they were amazed, and they didn't
know how to handle it.
And then I think about the stirrings of His heart
  when He heard the rumor of the great revival,
     the great baptizing going on by
        John Baptist.
       Something called Him
      to leave His life behind
    and come to the river
   AND TAKE HIS PLACE IN LINE.

Here was John,
 preaching a baptism of repentance
  for the forgiveness of the sins.
How deeply he probed!
   The depth of their false dependencies,

13

the depth of their self-righteousness was
totally exposed.
Think what it would be like to say to *Jewish* people,
God is able from these stones
to raise up children to Abraham.
That cut to the heart of their identity:
who they were
what they were.
He called into question the whole status quo,
bringing the judgment of God
upon their rationalizations
upon their casuistry
upon the way that they were carrying on life
as usual.
And Jesus came down
and joined the group
AND TOOK HIS PLACE IN LINE,
and in all of this
He identified with those He came
to save.
He entered into our humanity
as human
AND TOOK HIS PLACE IN LINE.
Folks,
do you know He
saves us
from within?

He comes to where we are
from within our humanity,
not outside.
And here we find Him identifying himself
with the purposes of God
and the needs of men
and dedicating himself
to the fulfillment of God's purposes
in His own life.

14

And then He was baptized.

I've come to believe that the baptism experience
    of Jesus
was a crucial event in His life.
I believe it was the time at which
        the growing inner consciousness
        of who He was
      and what He was
    was climaxed
    and sealed
      by the word of the Father
      and the anointing of the
      Holy Spirit.

Three of the Gospels speak
  specifically of the baptism experience.
They each tell us three things about it:
    The heavens were opened
    the Spirit descended
    and the voice of the Father was heard.

The heavens were opened.
  I'm not sure what that means;
  whether the clouds parted or what happened.
    But heaven, you know, is the abode of God
    and I think the statement means
    that the whole experience was God-ordained
      and was not just a product
    of Jesus' own imagination.
    It was nothing of His own doing.

The Spirit descended.
  Do you realize that during His early years
  Jesus had not performed any miracles
    had not told any great parables
    had not been a child prodigy.

He was a real, live, genuine, growing person
And did not enter His ministry
until He was filled with
the Spirit.
He, who was promised by the Spirit
and conceived by the Spirit
was filled with the Spirit.
We learn that later He did His works
in the power of the Spirit.
We also read in John's Gospel that before He returned
to the Father,
He breathed on them and said,
Receive the Holy Spirit.
(John 20:22)
And the Spirit that He gave
was His own Spirit, the Spirit in which
He himself
lived and loved and worked.
He was filled with the Spirit.
He was conscious, now,
of unique and special powers.
I believe that from the time of baptism
He was aware of the Spirit's anointing
and conscious of new and special powers.

The voice of the Father was heard.
Thou art my beloved Son;
with thee I am well pleased.
(Mark 1:11)
These two sayings of the Father to Jesus
come out of two different portions of scripture.
Thou art my beloved Son
comes from Psalm 2.
It was a coronation formula for the messianic
king of Israel.
When a new king was crowned, they would chant

the words of God
to their ruler:

Thou art my Son; this day have I begotten thee.
(v. 7, KJV)
As the years went by, national hopes grew
that someday some king would come
who would
actually fulfill God's will and purposes as
His Anointed One.
These stirrings of messianic hope
strengthened and increased
with each coronation
of a new king.

And I think that when He heard the Father say, "Thou
art my beloved Son,"
Jesus knew that He was to fulfill that messianic role.
I believe this was the time of anointing.
It was the time of empowerment.
It was the time when Jesus knew himself
to be
the anointed Son of God.
And then the Father said to Him,
With thee I am well pleased.
These words come from Isaiah 42,
the beginning of the servant songs,
the ordination formula
for the Suffering Servant of Yahweh:
Behold my servant, whom I uphold;
mine elect, in whom my soul delighteth;
I have put my spirit upon him:
he shall bring forth judgment
to the Gentiles. (Isa. 42:1, KJV)
It climaxes in Isaiah 53:
Who hath believed our report?
and to whom is the arm of the Lord revealed?

For he shall grow up before him as a tender plant,
and as a root out of a dry ground:
he hath no form nor comeliness;
and when we shall see him, there is no beauty
that we should desire him. He is despised
and rejected of men; a man of sorrows, and
acquainted with grief. (Isa. 53:1-3*a*, KJV)

We know that.
We've heard the *Messiah* sung.
But we need to see that Jesus saw
himself in this
portrait of the Suffering Servant
of Yahweh,
who fulfills His task
by deep identification with His people,
who fulfills the saving purposes
of God
in obedient love and suffering.

Now, I don't want to read too much into this passage,
but I believe this:
when Jesus left the waters of Jordan,
whatever had gone on inside Him before,
He knew who He was
He knew that He was Messiah
He knew He was the Son of God
and He knew that the Father
had called Him
to follow the path of the
Suffering Servant.

So Jesus leaves the Jordan River,
introduced into His ministry.
He has grown.
He has learned.
He has been ordained
anointed

filled with the Spirit.
He is aware that He is the Son
of God.
And He knows that His way is one of
suffering love.
But He is not ready yet.
As Mark puts it:

**The Spirit . . . drove him out
into the wilderness. And he
was . . . tempted
by Satan.** (Mark 1:12-13)

I have come to the conclusion
THAT WE CANNOT REALLY EVER UNDERSTAND THE
TEMPTATIONS OF JESUS
UNLESS WE SEE THEM IN THE CONTEXT OF THE BAPTISM.

We have looked at Jesus growing through the years
coming to His baptism
anointed with the Spirit
open and yielded to the Father's will.
Now the Spirit drives Him into
the wilderness
where He is tempted by the devil
for 40 days and 40 nights.
I think we should understand
that 40 days and 40 nights
is a special term to mean
a long time.
It is a rough equivalent to our word *month*.
Let's see,
wasn't Moses 40 days and 40 nights on the mount?
Didn't Noah see it rain for 40 days and 40 nights?
Elijah went 40 days and 40 nights in
the strength
of the food God gave him.
Wasn't Jonah in the belly of the whale
40 days and 40 nights?

Well, no, but it seemed
like it!
And here in the wilderness
for this long time
He was tempted.
You know how
the questions keep coming up in Sunday School class:
How could Jesus be tempted?
How could His temptation be real?
I tell you this much,
it is no good for us to see the temptation of Jesus
as a little three-act drama
played out in the presence of
rodents
jackals
gophers
snakes
and lizards
in the high desert above the
Jordan River.
Do not view the temptations as some drama
in which the bad guy loses
the good guy wins
with the curtain closing as
Satan slinks away defeated
and Jesus marches away triumphant
conquering and to conquer.
THAT IS NOT A GOOD WAY TO VIEW THEM.
Real and awful struggle was taking place; it was
struggle between
heaven and earth, battle between God and Satan. In
the crucible was
Jesus.
And the temptations never quit! They continued
deeply
and consistently all through His life

20

                              clear to the end.
                   On that desperate night
                              He cried,
                         If thou art willing,
                         remove this cup from me.
                         (Luke 22:42)
                   On that awful morning
                              He cried,
                         My God, my God,
                         why hast thou forsaken me?
                         (Mark 15:34)
       All the way along there were
            deep and probing trials.
What we see is a real
                   live
                   genuine
                   person
                        anointed of the Spirit
                        aware of His relationships;
                              BUT IN THE WILDERNESS,
                              WHO HE WAS
                              AND WHAT HE WAS TO DO
                              WERE DEEPLY SEARCHED
                                        AND TESTED.

I want to talk about that.
       First, He was tempted to doubt
       that validity of the Father's word to Him.
       It was the question Am I really the Son of God?
Look at it this way:
    He emerges out of baptism
       the Spirit comes in the form of a dove
          the voice of the Father is heard
             "Thou art my beloved Son."
                   Forty days and 40 nights go by
                        and the next voice you hear

                              21

is the voice of the devil saying,
If you are the Son of God . . .
Do you understand that?
If Jesus never said to himself,
"Am I really who I think I am?"
then He was not tempted in
all points
as I am
or we are.
I wonder if there are any of us
who have not heard the voice of the Father
at the altar on a Sunday night
after a great service where we're all singing,
I'm going through, Jesus,
I'll pay the price whatever others do,
And everybody's blessed half to death
and nobody wants to go home
and the voice of the Father is clear.
Thou art my son.
Anybody not understand that?
If you have never experienced such things
then just go home and fast and pray
that someday you will;
Because those are some of the beautiful times.
At such times the voice of the Father is crystal clear:
"Thou art my son!"

And then there is Monday.
Anybody not understand that?
I have to say to you that when I am in vivid awareness
of the presence of God and my relationship with Him,
the devil can't touch me with a 10-foot pole.
You know
I'm praising the Lord
and get thee behind me, Satan!
It's those other times

that are bad for me.
The times when the Father's voice is *not* heard and the
voice of Satan
is loud and clear: "Yea, hath God said?"
I believe deeply that Jesus understands
the inner feelings we cannot avoid:
Are we who we say we are?
Come to think of it, this is the very temptation
our first father met in the Garden of Eden.
In Mark's narrative of the temptation experience,
he says that Jesus was
driven of the Spirit into the wilderness
and was with the wild beasts. (cf. Mark 1:12-13)
When I read that phrase my mind goes back to Eden
where our first father was with the beasts
in a garden of plenty
in an intimate fellowship with his Father.
And there
in that garden of plenty
the voice of the tempter was saying:
Oh?
Is that right?
Has God indeed said?

And our first father's temptation
was to doubt the validity of his relationship with
his Father.
And the temptation of our Elder Brother, Jesus,
was to doubt the validity of his relationship with
His Father.
And the temptation of all the little brothers and sisters
is to doubt the validity of their relationship with
the Father.
The beauty of it is
that our Lord Jesus,
in the wilderness
desolate and bare,

23

never let go His trust in His Father.
Amen!

He'd been fasting
and wrestling
and hassling
without any supporting words
without any strokes
no warm fuzzies,
in a desolate
barren
wilderness.
And He never let go His faith in His Father
nor His trust in the Father's love and care for Him.
I thank God that we may share in the victory
that our Lord won there.
By His Spirit there is help for us
not to let go our trust in the Father's care
nor our trust in and our relationship with Him
at the times in our lives
of failure
or distress
or testing
or bleakness
or barrenness
or aloneness.
What's the fundamental issue?
Don't let go your faith in the Father.
Don't lose trust in your relationship with Him.

I think the second temptation underneath the episodes
of bread
and Temple
and kingdoms of the world
relates to Jesus' understanding of His ministry.
At the Jordan, He heard His Father say, "With thee I
am well pleased."

24

He knew then His task was one of servanthood
    and suffering.
I believe that in every temptation Jesus faced
  there was the fundamental temptation
        to turn away
            from the path of suffering love
            to which his Father had called Him,
  (That's where we're tempted, too, isn't it?)
  the temptation to avoid the Cross and
        to turn away
            from the path of servanthood
                and suffering,
            to find some other way
            to fulfill the Father's purpose.
                Let's think about that in
                    the temptations
                of Jesus and in ours.

*Then Jesus was led up by the Spirit into the
wilderness to be tempted by the devil. And he
fasted forty days and forty nights, and
afterward he was hungry. And the tempter
came and said to him, "If you are the Son of
God, command these stones to become loaves
of bread." But he answered, "It is written,
'Man shall not live by bread alone, but by
every word that proceeds from the mouth of
God.'"*
Matt. 4:1-4

2

To Eat or Not to Eat

Each of the temptations indicate that Jesus
was conscious of possessing special powers.
He was tempted to do what ordinary people could
never do.
**The tempter came and said to him,
"If you are the Son of God,
command these stones to become
loaves of bread . . .
throw yourself down . . .
All these I will give you . . . "**
(Matt. 4:3, 6, 9)
Now, I have never been tempted to use my power to
turn stones into bread.

Have you?

Turning bread into stones
is another matter.
That I can do.
And you just better believe I have never been tempted
to leap off the pinnacle of the Temple.
If you ever hear that I died
by falling from a high place
you call Sherlock Holmes or Dick Tracy
or somebody
because it was murder.
I did not leap.
I was pushed!
I suppose I have had my own little temptations
to gain the glory of the world,
even though my world is not all that glorious.
But Jesus' temptations reveal His awareness of power,
and His
temptations were precisely at the point of the use of
His power.
Here is the One who is to be the Messiah of
the world,
and He is starving to death in the wilderness.
Here's a great way to start your ministry:
go off into the wilderness
where nobody can find you
and die of starvation.
He has the power that can turn stones into bread
and He doesn't use it.
I'm wondering why.
Why didn't He do it?
We need to keep in mind that Jesus didn't always fast.
John the Baptist fasted a lot.
He didn't get invited to very
many weddings.
He was not exactly on the dinner
party circuit.

But Jesus was.
Did you know that?
And He loved sinners.
And they loved Him.
Jesus didn't always fast.
He was, in fact, characterized as a glutton and a
winebibber.
Surely He only ate health foods:
Granola
Trail-mix
Gatorade.
Jesus did not live His life in austerity.
But here at this crucial testing point, feeling the
incredible pain of
40 days and 40 nights worth of hunger,
He refused to use His power for himself.
Well, why didn't He?
You know, Israel was led into the wilderness
and fed.

Jesus, the embodiment of Israel,
was led into the wilderness

and not fed.
His needs were real.
He had the power to take care of himself,
and He didn't do it.

You see, Jesus had a gift
a power
but He never turned it in upon himself to meet
His own needs.
We all know of people who have special gifts
God seems to use and bless in a wonderful way.
Too often when those gifts begin to be used and
affirmed in the church,
they get an agent
and you can't afford them anymore.

They hit the entertainment circuit, make
    the bigtime,
  and something precious is lost.
Or they write books and go on the road to peddle them.
            I'm a little sensitive at this point,
            But keep those orders
                 coming in, folks!
I'm really not kidding. I struggle with it myself.
  I get upset when publishers don't push my books as
    much as I want them to.
      And then the Lord talks to me and says,
        Now, wait just a minute.
        What's happening to your motives?
And we all know musicians God blesses and uses in
    ministry to the body of believers.
Then they make records and must sell them.
They come in early to set up
and just happen to have 40 copies on special.
    Somewhere in here, ministry becomes
      show business.
  What began as a gift
      a power
      a special talent
      some unique, precious something
    has turned inward
        and become commercialized.
And I'm thinking that right at this point,
Jesus resisted this very temptation.
    What bothers me is that we all want bread
           or money and need it.
  I want bread and you want bread
    and we'll use whatever legitimate means we can
      to get it.
    You know,
    I need a raise in salary.
    I've earned it after all these years.

Who deserves it more than I?
Besides, I have real needs. And so do you.
You can tell when pastors need to move on.
It is when they have lost their love for the people
and are thinking in terms of salary
                              or parsonages
                                   or whatever.
                 A subtle shift has taken place
                 from self-giving
                                   to self-protecting.
That's the heart of this whole business.
So, one element underlying Jesus' temptations
                 is His own personal need,
                 His own sense of fulfillment.

Every now and then I hear someone say,
        It's bad stewardship
        NOT to capitalize on the gifts God has given.
                                   Ever heard that?
        Good stewardship means, then,
        we ought to use our gifts to make as much money
                              as we can.
                 Something in me says,
                 "That's capitulation to the
                                   profit system!"
I think I read somewhere that the gifts are given for
building up of the body. (See Eph. 4.)
Jesus struggled with this very issue.
                 He won for us the victory we may share
                 and He did it when He was just about to
                                   starve to death.
                              Now that helps me.
It brings me back to see that whatever God has given,
        whatever special gifts
                 or powers
                 or charisma

or ministry
whatever it is, it is given for giving.
If the motive moves away from giving
to getting,
something precious is gone.

There's another issue in the temptation to turn stones
into bread.
Not only are Jesus' own personal needs involved,
but the needs of men.
Did you know that Jesus had the power to feed the
world?
Did you know that?
You know as well as I do that the man who can feed
the world can rule the world.
So the temptation Jesus faced
was to give His ministry
to meeting the legitimate needs of the world.
And they are legitimate, aren't they?
In the prayer our Lord taught us, we say,
Give us this day our daily bread.
Jesus lived in a starving world,
poverty was everywhere.
He knew as well as anyone that there is little good
in talking to people about their souls
while their stomachs are growling.
But in the face of all that, I see Him turn away
from legitimate human needs,
needs He could have filled,
to take the lonely way
to Calvary's cross
to die.
Can you see that temptation?
It's clearly revealed in the way John records the feeding
of the five thousand;
when it was all over and they were well fed, Jesus
perceived that

"they were about to come and take him by force to
make him king,"
and He heard again the tempter's words —
Turn these stones into bread.
He fed the multitudes and they wanted to make Him
a king.
Do you know how to be a king?
Feed the people.
Do you want to win the world?
Feed the world.

So — to eat or not to eat
that is the question.
to feed or not to feed
that is the question.
No — that is not the question!
To obey or not to obey, *that* is the
question.
Listen to the Old Testament passage Jesus quoted
to Satan:
**All the commandment which I command you
this day
you shall be careful to do. . . .
And you shall remember all the way which the
Lord your God has led you. . . .
And he humbled you and let you hunger
and fed you with manna, . . . that he might
make you know
that man does not live by bread alone,
but that man lives by everything
that proceeds out of the mouth of the
Lord. (Deut. 8:1-3)**
When it comes right down to it, the fundamental
issue is
obedience to the Word of the Father.
Sure, I have temptations to meet my own needs.

Sometimes I feel like the village pump;
   everybody who comes along just pumps a little more
     out of me.
   Did you ever feel like the sick cannibal
      who was fed up on people?
        I wrote a book called
          We Really Do Need Each Other
        and I'm working on a sequel—
          Would Everybody Please Leave Me Alone!
            Does anybody not understand that?
I have needs and you have needs,
            real
            genuine
            gnawing
            growling
            yearning needs.

Jesus had needs, too.
And sometimes He met them. He did not always fast.
   Sometimes He did not meet them.
But whether He did or didn't,
     for himself or for others,
         the one controlling word
            was the Word of His Father.
I guess that's the hard thing for us, isn't it,
   to keep getting our direction
     NOT
        from our own needs
        or the needs of others,
   but getting our direction by obedience
          to the Word of the Father,
          who sometimes feeds us
          with manna
          and sometimes lets us
            go hungry
           that we may know
           what it is we really live by.

*Then the devil took him to the holy city, and
set him on the pinnacle of the temple, and
said to him, "If you are the Son of God,
throw yourself down; for it is written, 'He
will give his angels charge of you,' and 'On
their hands they will bear you up, lest you
strike your foot against a stone.'" Jesus said
to him, "Again it is written, 'You shall not
tempt the Lord your God.'"*
Matt. 4:5-7

3

Don't Expect a Miracle

I believe that the temptations of Jesus
   were not endured just for our benefit.
     They were His own.

                        Let me run that by again.
The temptations of Jesus were not for our benefit.
That does not mean, of course,
                  that we do not profit from them.
But He was not tempted on our behalf.
The temptation experience was His.
And the struggle was His.
   He was not role-playing
      or play-acting.
   He was not saying to himself,
   Those who follow Me will be tempted,
   so I'd best be doing this

so they will know how to act.
I think many have the feeling
                that Jesus went through these experiences
                as our Great Example
                as our Pattern
                        so that we will understand how to
                        resist the
                        tempter in our time of trial.
                                Of course, He does become
                                a pattern for our lives,
                                        after the fact.

But the life He lived
        the testings He experienced
        the hungers
        the yearnings
        the trials and the obedience
                were all His.
I believe that it is precisely because the temptation
        was *His* struggle
                His battle
                        His own inner life test
                                that it becomes so helpful for us.

But there is not a one-to-one ratio
        between His temptations and ours.
We know He was tempted in all points as we are.
        That is true.
                        But in another sense it is not true.
                        He did not experience the temptations
                        of a middle-aged married man of the
                                twentieth century.
                        He did not experience the temptations
                        of a single woman of college age.
                                Do you know what I mean?

        But He did experience
        all that it means to be totally human

35

and be tempted in all the ways humans are
tempted.
He entered totally into our human situation.
The life He lived
was His own.
The faith that He had in His Father
was His own.
That is why He knows me so well and shares my
struggles from inside.

We have talked
about the temptations in general
and turning stones into bread in particular.
Let's talk now about the temptation—His own real
temptation—
to leap off the pinnacle of the Temple.
**Then the devil took him to the holy city,
and set him on the pinnacle of the temple,
and said to him, "If you are the Son of God,
throw yourself down; for it is written,
'He will give his angels charge of you,'
and
'On their hands they will bear you up,
lest you strike your foot against a stone.'"
Jesus said to him, "Again it is written, 'You
shall not tempt the Lord your God.'"**
(Matt. 4:5-7)
I have been wondering
how in the world it could have been any valid
temptation
for Jesus to leap off the pinnacle of the Temple.
You know, I shared with you a true insight
into my life and character in the second chapter.
Of all the temptations I have ever had,
that has not been one of them!
How could it be a temptation to Jesus?

Maybe it will help to view it in light of
                contemporary
                Jewish
                    messianic expectation.
We have said that Jesus emerged from the waters of
        Jordan
        aware of His unique relationship to God,
        aware that the task to which He had been called
            was the task of messianic, suffering love.
                        But we know, also,
                        that He did not live in a vacuum.
                        There were contemporary
                                messianic expectations.
We know that Satan quoted from Psalm 91:11-12.
Let's just go back and read it:
            For he will give his angels charge of you
            to guard you in all your ways.

            On their hands they will bear you up,
            lest you dash your foot against a stone.
Then it goes on to say:
            You will tread on the lion and the adder,
            the young lion and the serpent you will
            trample under foot.

            Because he cleaves to me in love, I will
            deliver him; I will protect him, because he
            knows my name.

            When he calls to me, I will answer him; I
            will be with him in trouble, I will rescue him
            and honor him.

            With long life I will satisfy him, and show
            him my salvation.
            (Ps. 91:13-16)
The scholars of Jesus' day
    looked at this psalm as a messianic psalm
    referring to the Anointed One who would come in the
    latter days.

One of their commentaries says,
>"When King Messiah is revealed, He comes
>and stands upon the roof of the holy place.
>Then He will announce to the Israelites
>and say,
>'Ye poor, the time of your redemption
has come.'"

Let's step back and take a look at this.
It is time for the morning sacrifice.
Worshipers are gathering in the courtyard,
filled with expectation.
Suddenly, appearing from the Temple pinnacle
comes the Man from heaven.
Surrounded by His angels, He descends
into the midst
of His worshiping followers.
Their dreams have come true.
Their prayers have been answered;
the Messiah has come.
I tell you,
they will rise up, and follow
Him forever.
Well, at least until tomorrow.

I have read that the masses are hungry for miracle
for mystery
for authority
and I believe it.
They are hungry for gurus
who have charisma
who have authority
who can reveal mystery
who can do magic.
One of the temptations of Jesus
was to feed this hunger, to accomplish His Father's
purpose

38

by catering to this desire for miracle, for mystery,
and authority.
In the young among whom I am privileged to live,
there is a profound desire for a Christian life that is
out of this world
fantastic
something out of the ordinary.
There is a fundamental resistance to
day by day
ordinary
do your homework
eat right
go to bed
be nice
kind of religion.
Now, that's true, isn't it?
That's dull.
It has no basic appeal.
What they want is a miracle.

Several years ago, I knew a man who claimed a gift
of healing.
People gathered at his house to get their legs equalized.
I don't know what genetic problem caused it,
but an astonishing number found out
that one leg was shorter than the other.
This man had a tremendous ability
to lengthen the short leg!
One of the young fellows at school was all caught up
in this.
He had been to a meeting and found that one leg
was just about two inches shorter than the other.
They put him in a chair
put his legs out
the healer prayed
and that short leg came right out
and he was OK.

We were at a student/faculty committee
meeting when this student came in
and shared the exciting news
of his lengthened leg.
I never will forget the president's response—
no change of expression—
"Well, for goodness sake,
Isn't that interesting."
And we went on with the meeting.
I've had a special liking for him ever since.
He had the ability to say,
"Hmm. Ain't it a wonder."
He didn't give too much credence
to this display of healing power.
Why didn't he?
I believe it was because the miracle was obviously
sensational.
Its end was not discipleship, but amazement.
For that matter, I have not been able
to recover from what happened in Jonestown, Guyana.
I keep thinking of the normal,
ordinary
good people
who hungered for peace
and security.
They wanted affirmation.
They wanted love.
They had real
deep
genuine needs,
and they found someone who loved them like
nobody else,
who had authority
and charisma.
And they sold their freedom
for the miraculous

for the mysterious
for the authoritarian,
and they followed him
all the way
to death.

I cannot get that out of my head.
And when you think of how many people
are capitalizing on the hunger for the miraculous . . .
Out our way, we have a TV preacher,
I forget his name
I've heard more about him
than I've seen him.
He has people come up to be healed, or
"slain in the Spirit."
His white-suited cohorts are standing around
and he stretches out his hand
and the people fall down
just laid out in the Lord
slain in the Spirit.

Ain't it a wonder?
And I wonder whose real needs are being met?
For whose glory is the performance?
What do the miracles mean?
It helps me to know that Jesus faced these very issues.
He had to answer the questions
"All right, who am I?
How am I going to fulfill my ministry?"
We know about healers.
We know about sensational leaders who say,
You've got to get the attention of the world.
You've got to have a miracle or what looks
like one.
This is what folks want.
Give them what they want.
But Jesus turned away
from those expectations

and took the lonely path
to Calvary's cross
to die.

Once in a while I remember that,
and when I do it scares me a little.

There's another dimension to this temptation
that I think is even more fundamental.
I believe that Jesus interpreted the meaning
of the temptation by the way He answered
the tempter.
Again, it is the temptation
to test the validity of His relationship
with His Father.
It is as though Satan said to Him something like this:
"If You are the Son of God,
then You have a claim on God.
Whatever happens, You will be saved
from harm."
And in order to test and show that God was present
with Him,
Jesus was tempted to put His Father in a position
that would make it necessary for Him to respond
to the trustful act of Jesus.
He was tempted to *use* His Father,
to manipulate Him in order to prove that He was
the Father's Son.
Jesus understood the temptation that way.
He quoted from Deuteronomy:
You shall not put the Lord your God to the
test, as you tested him at Massah.
You shall diligently keep the commandments
of the Lord your God, and his testimonies,
and his
statutes, which he has commanded you.
And you shall do what is right and good

in sight of the Lord.
(Deut. 6:16-18*a*)

Did you hear that?
You shall not put the Lord your God to the
test, as you tested him at Massah.
The Massah incident comes out of Exodus 17:

All the congregation of the people of Israel
moved on from the wilderness . . . and
camped at Rephidim;
but there was no water for the people
to drink.
Therefore, the people found fault
with Moses,
and said, "Give us water to drink." And
Moses said to
them, "Why do you find fault with me? Why
do you put the Lord to the proof?"
But the people thirsted there for water, and
the people murmured against Moses, and said,
"Why did you bring us up out of Egypt,
to kill us
and our children and our cattle with thirst?"
So Moses cried to the Lord, "What shall
I do
with this people? They are almost ready to
stone me."
And the Lord said to Moses, " . . . Behold,
I will
stand before you there on the rock at Horeb;
and you shall
strike the rock, and water shall come out of
it, that the people may drink." . . .
And he called the name of the place
Massah and Meribah, because of the
faultfinding of the children of Israel, . . .
Listen to this:

43

and because they put the Lord to the
proof by saying, "Is the Lord among us
or not?"
(Exodus 17:1-7)

What a question!
Is the Lord among us or not?
Am I a child of God, or not?
Given our Western way of thinking, the conclusion
is natural:
How can you prove you are a child of God?
And we get an "if-then" syndrome going:
it goes like this:
If the Lord is among us and we really have the
Holy Spirit,
then a-b-c-d-e will follow.
But maybe we are not seeing a-b-c-d-e.
Where is God?
Over there some superchurch is going gung ho
and over here where we are . . . nothing!
Have you ever noticed that most of what
the Holy Spirit is doing is where somebody
else is?
It's discouraging, isn't it?
. . . and over here where we are, things aren't
quite so exciting.
Is God with us, or not?
Is He with us?
What's the matter with us?
And when we are at that point, we are terribly
vulnerable.
Our church
(I think I'll just say *our church* with a small *c*,
and that includes the whole bunch of us),
our church
doesn't seem to be growing all that much,
and some other parts of the Kingdom

44

are spreading like wildfire,
and we are wondering what has gone wrong.
We are at a most dangerous and vulnerable
place,
aren't we?

Right at this point, we begin to ask questions:
Where is the glory of the bygone day?
Where is God working?
Are we His children?
What needs to be happening
to demonstrate that God is indeed among us?
We are tempted to fulfill expectation
to cater to miracle,
to mystery
to authority.
One way or another, we've got to demonstrate our
status with God.
And underneath is the question hidden and unspoken:
Is God with us, or not?

Now, the worst of this temptation is
that it is done with scripture
and it takes place in the temple of God.
Think about that a minute.
Where is the great inner strength of Jesus
about himself
and His task?

It's in the scripture
and it's in the temple of God.
And scripture is used by both Satan
and
Jesus.

The first temptation was
"Command these stones to become . . . bread."
Satan didn't back it up with scripture,
but Jesus answered him, "It is written . . . "

45

Satan picks up on that and says,
 "All right, then do this . . .
 because it is written . . . "
Jesus answered, "No! because it is written . . . "
SATAN USED SCRIPTURE AGAINST JESUS,
AND JESUS USED SCRIPTURE AGAINST SATAN,
 and sometimes that's a little scary.
Here is the crucial difference:
 Satan *used* scripture—Jesus trusted His Father and
 lived under the
 authority of scripture in obedience to His
 Father's Word.
In one sense,
 if Jesus had leaped from the Temple
 He would have been doing it as an act of trust
 in His Father's promise.
 He could have leaped singing, "Standing on the
 promises of God!"
Well, let's look back at Psalm 91:11-12:
 He will give his angels charge of you . . .
 On their hands they will bear you up,
 lest you dash your foot against a stone.
 Is that true or false?
 He will . . . guard you in all your ways.
 Is that true or false?
 Is God's
 Word the truth?
 And if His Word is the truth
 and we are His people
 and we trust His promise
 then we can say
"Take God at His word
 and step out on the promises of God."

 Well, is the Word of God
 true or false?
 It is true, of course.

Listen to some scriptures:

> Bring ye all the tithes into the storehouse . . .
> and prove me now herewith, saith the Lord
>   of hosts,
> if I will not open you the windows of heaven,
> and pour you out a blessing,
> that there shall not be room enough to
>   receive it.

(Mal. 3:10, KJV)

> And other such good things in
>   the passage
> as are added by the pastor when
> the offerings are down.
>
> *Well, is that promise true or false?*
> Does God keep His Word?

It matters terribly how we answer these questions and
how we respond to the promise.

One thing we can do and have done is step out on the
promise in obedience and look for riches and
blessings to follow.

Do you remember a brother
who not too long ago was ministering among us
    saying,
"What we need to do is tithe on the amount
of income we want to receive. God loves
    Cadillacs.
How much money do you want? Start tithing on
that amount—you can't lose."

Here's the premise:
God keeps His Word.

> What is His Word?
> It is spiritual law.
> Tithe, and you will receive.
> Give, and it will be given unto you.
> Do you want to be given unto?
> Then, give.

47

God honors His Word.
He loves to keep His word.
He loves for His people to step out on
His word.
Oh, I can hear the TV preachers now, can't you?
I can hear a few un-TV preachers, too.

*So, keep those cards and letters
coming in, folks, and we'll keep
this program on the air and
have a worldwide ministry, and
I'll send you a free copy of my
book by return mail.*

Well, does God keep His Word or not?

**Train up a child in the way he should go:
and when he is old, he will not depart from
it. (Prov. 22:6, KJV)**

Is that true?
All right, then,
discipline
and trust God.
You will have the model
family.

*Does the Bible mean what it says,
or doesn't it?*

*Is God true to His promise
or not?*

Step out on the promise.
Act and God will come through.
You know what this sounds like?

If you do your part,
then God is obligated to do His part.
He has promised and He will fulfill.
If you act,
then He will respond.

*I hope we get out of this all right,
don't you?*

48

Hang on!
If you take Him at His word,
   if you believe and not doubt,
      you have pulled the levers that activate the
      power of God.
   He will come through for you.
And Jesus said,
   You shall not tempt the Lord your God.
I remember talking to a pastor friend of mine
who went through a time of darkness and despair.
He had no sense of God. I mean, God was nowhere.
         And if you do not understand that,
         just tune out.
Have you ever had those times when
      nothing speaks to you in a book you have
      and there's not a verse in the Bible that helps.
      There's just nothing, nowhere.
He was in one of those times.
And he said,
     "I'm going into my study and I'm not coming
     out until I know God is real."
  He went into his study
  locked the door
    cut off the phone
    and began to pray
         and nothing happened.
So he prayed some more, crying in distress,
   "God, if you are real and I am your child,
     then, let a breeze blow
       let a piece of paper fall
       let something . . . anything . . . happen
       so I'll know.
I'm not leaving here until I know.
Oh, God, do something."
        You know the result of that.
        Nothing happened.

No papers gently shifted off
the desk.
No cobweb swayed from the
ceiling.
Nothing.
Finally, when he was too tired to pray anymore,
he relaxed. He suddenly saw himself and what he
was doing and began to laugh —
and he was OK.

Do you see what he was
doing?
The same thing we do.
He was manipulating God, forcing an answer to the
question
Is God with me or not?

Folks,
do you know that with all the clout and power Jesus
had, **He lived all His life in obedience and trust in His
Father, and He never put His Father to the test.**
He went all the way to Calvary,
and He could have called ten thousand angels.
Just think about that.
I think this is the significant element in the
temptation because Jesus quoted this scripture in
answer to the tempter:
**You shall not put the Lord your God to the
test, as you tested him at Massah.**
What was the Massah temptation?
Is the Lord among us or not?
The if-then syndrome:
If you are the Son of God, *then* . . .
put God to the test.
And Jesus lived His life
in good times and bad times
in affirmation times and denial times

in high times and low times
in fasting and feasting
in acceptance and rejection.
He lived His life trusting His Father
as the scripture said in Deuteronomy:
**diligently keeping the commandments of the
Lord . . . and doing what is right and good in
the sight of the Lord.** (cf. Deut. 6:17-18)
And not saying,
Is the Lord among us or not?

That helps me!

And what I hear out of this passage is:
Do not say,
"Is the Lord among us or not?"
Do not say, "Is God with me?"
Don't say that.
Obey God.
Trust God.
Do what is right and good in the sight of
the Lord.
Don't ask for something to demonstrate
that He is with you.
Believe it: He is with you.

I understand the hunger for magic
for miracle
for mystery
for authority
But Jesus never put His Father to the test.
You shall not tempt the Lord your God.
Do you see what it does to God when we put Him to
the test?
"If you will – then God will."
It makes God into an impersonal power
and makes no reference to His holy, personal will.
"If you do your part,

then God is obligated to do His."
When I hear that, something rises up inside me to say,
Oh,
Wait a minute!
Who is who in this business?
Sometimes I see a little slogan posted around that says,
Expect a Miracle!
If you have those posters in your church,
I hope you will still love me and understand that I'd
   like you to go and take them down
      and try not to ruin the paint.
Expect a miracle!
Expect a miracle?
Not if it creates a demand that
      divine power respond to your command.
         Not if it makes faith a lever
            to manipulate divine activity.
At a time when our college leader was seriously ill
      and failing, students began to rally and to say,
         We can't have this.
         We need him.
         We have got to bind together,
            trust God,
               and get him healed.
Do you understand that?
         God can get glory out of this
               and we have to get him healed.
         Let's bind together.
         Let's get a prayer chain.
         Let's get hold of God
               and get him healed.
I did a lot of thinking in those days about such things.
I think that is partly what has brought about
   these thoughts and probings in my own heart
   about this temptation of Jesus.
You see,

if God is with us
and we believe,
>*then God will heal.*

Claim His promise,
step out on His promise,
>*then God will act.*

What's hard is, I believe all that.
BUT WHEN IT BECOMES A MANIPULATION OF GOD,
>WE ARE PUTTING HIM TO THE TEST.

And I will tell you what I came to believe during
>>those days:
>>If the college leader is healed
>>>Jesus is Lord!
>>If our school flourishes
>>>Jesus is Lord!
>>If it declines
>>>Jesus is Lord!
>>If our church grows
>>>Jesus is Lord!
>>If it does not grow
>>>Jesus is Lord!

>He is in charge here.
>And our faith is not dependent
>>upon the miraculous work of God
>>>to demonstrate that He is among us.

So I want you to get another poster to put up
in place of the one you took down:
>>>Don't Expect a Miracle!

Our oldest girl is brain-damaged
>>retarded
>>and institutionalized.

And we've gone the route of expecting miracles.
We've gone the route of healing services and anointings.
You name it; we've done it.
>>>And nothing has happened
>>>**and Jesus is Lord!**

I know people all around the place who want a miracle,
        And I think it can be a cop-out.
Don't expect a miracle.
    Obey God!

                    **You shall not put the Lord
                    to the test.**
Don't expect a miracle,
                *but keep the commandments of the
                                            Lord
                and do what is right in the sight
                of the Lord.*
I believe that this is precisely the kind of faith
    Jesus had.
I believe it is the kind of faith that trusts the
    Father to do His gracious will, with or
    without miracles.
It is faith that trusts and believes and does
    not manipulate.
He is in charge here.
We may trust Him,
    we may not manipulate Him.

                *Trusting as the moments fly;
                Trusting as the days go by;
                Trusting Him what e'er befall;
                Trusting Jesus, that is all.*

God so loved the world, that he gave his only
begotten Son, that whosoever believeth in him
should not perish, but have everlasting life."

(John 3:16, KJV)

4

The Power and the Glory

Again, the devil took him to a very high
mountain, and showed him all the kingdoms of
the world and the glory of them;
and he said to him, "All these I will give
you, if you will fall down and worship me."
(Matt. 4:8-9)

You know, Jesus came because of the world.
Isn't that why He came?

It is the world that God loved
the world into which Jesus came
and the world into which we are sent.

Go ye into all the world, and preach
the gospel to every creature. (Mark 16:15, KJV)

He came to save the world,
   and right here the world was before Him,
      virtually laid in the palm of His hand.
                Just think about that.

Satan showed Him all the kingdoms of the world
and the glory of them.

        I have often wondered what kind of
                      panoramic view
          Jesus had, as in His mind He stood there
          on the mountain.

He was on a towering peak
   where He could see
      all the kingdoms of the world:
      all the marching armies
      all the conquering parades
      all the might and wisdom
      all the power and the glory.

        They were right there at His feet.
        And He turned away from the whole
      picture and took the lonely way
   to Calvary's cross
to die.

        **"All these I will give you, if you will fall
        down and worship me."** (Matt. 4:9)

I don't think Satan was actually saying to Jesus,
     Call me God.
        No way could Jesus be tempted to call
                 Satan God.

Jesus knows that Satan isn't God.
  And Satan knows that he is not God.
        I think that's his problem.
        He isn't God and he knows it,
             but he wants to be!

For Jesus to call Satan God
wouldn't change anything but a term.

The real issue is a matter of compromise.

I don't know if that's the best word
but let's begin with it.

An issue of compromise: THE RECOGNITION OF THE

REALITY

OF SATAN'S LORDSHIP IN THIS

WORLD.

In the confrontation Jesus was tempted
to affirm the reality of Satan's lordship in the world
to recognize it
to work with it
to accept it.

It was the temptation to recognize and accept
our fallenness,
to accept the gray in the world
to have the good judgment to work with that
reality
and accept things the way they are.

It was the temptation to say yes to the lordship of
Satan in this world and to fulfill His kingdom
ministry by working within Satan's domain.

You know, there is a sense in which
Satan is, indeed, lord of this world.
He exercises an awesome
power in our world.

However, I will tell you what I have come to believe:
Satan's dominion in our world
is the great delusion.
His lordship rests on a lie
and his house is a house of cards.
The power that Satan has
is the power of unreality
the power of delusion

57

the power of the lie.
Have you ever had thoughts like these:

    Do you suppose Christianity is just a great fantasy
    that has been passed on from generation to
                         generation?
    What if we discover that the whole thing is a great
    myth that has been perpetuated through the
                         centuries?
                Anybody not thought that?
                     Of course not.

Here is the truth:
    there is a great fantasy,
    there is a great delusion
        that has been perpetuated through the centuries.
        It is the delusion of the reality
        of Satan's lordship in this world.
I think the testing,
    the tempting that Jesus faced there in the wilderness
    was the test we all have in our ministry.
        It is the test of the degree to which we will
        capitulate to the inevitabilities of the fallen
        system and work within it to fulfill the purposes
        of God.

Let me share what I read from a book on Luke,
The Compassionate Christ, by Walter Russell Bowie:

        *In the thrilling consciousness of his
        mission which had illumined him at his
        baptism, his spirit had been exalted. But
        always after exaltation, there come the
        crowding questions as to where the road
        runs next. Can actual life continue on the
        level of the heavenly vision? Or must it
        come down into the valley of compromis-
        ing choices if it is to find the realistic
        way ahead.*

Oh, I hear that phrase.
Do you hear it?
*The realistic way ahead—
the way of compromising
choices.*

I think that points to the heart of who we are and
what we are.
And I don't have any answers,
but I really am struggling with the
problem.
As denominations or colleges or groups, we certainly
are pragmatic, aren't we?
We really do bow down at the shrine of what works.
And when something works,
we have a marvelous ability to
analyze it
rationalize it
sanctify it
and incorporate it into God's program in the
world.
I know we have our dreams, but really—
we have to face facts.
We have to be practical.
Somebody has to pay the bills.
What I just said is true.
We *do* have our visions
and we *do* have to face facts.
We live in that tension.
We are in the world
and we live within the system of the world
and we live in a fallen world.
We understand, don't we,
that the church, *as an institution*,
partakes of the fallenness that characterizes all
the institutions in a fallen world.
God knows that.

59

He has always worked in the midst of systems and
                                    governments
        all kinds of governments
        all kinds of cultures
            as He has gathered together His ragtag
                                        followers.
And somehow, in the midst of our humanness
                        and weaknesses
                        and failures
He does His redeeming work in the world.
In the meantime, we hassle with the systems
                    and work within the systems
            where there are policies
                that sometimes are destructive to others.
    When you're in charge of the policies
    and they work to your benefit, then
                            thank God for policies!

    Isn't it wonderful that when you want to make
        a shift that might hurt somebody,
        there is always a policy you can bring out
        so you don't have to face the fact of hurting
                                    people.
        Our ability to rationalize decisions in our favor
                            is amazing!
    There's not one of us who doesn't understand that!
I've thought about that in connection with college
                                    revivals.
I've taught at a college since 1960 and
    been a college chaplain for a long time.
I've noticed something through the years.
    This relates to my world, maybe you can relate it
                                    to yours.
College revivals are always for students.
                    Have you ever noticed that?
Who is to repent at revival time?
            Students are to repent.

When there are hassles with policies and regulations,
who is to repent and have a good attitude?
      Students.
When they come in September and class schedules
                don't work out,

who is to have the good attitude?
      Students.
And if they don't have a good attitude,
   then we need to have a revival,
      so students can repent.
I've noticed that when you have confession times,
   hardly ever does the faculty confess.
   Seldom is there an admission that an exam may
                  not be valid;

    students must adjust.
   Hardly ever does college leadership say,
     You know, that was one bad decision,
     and we need to ask the students to forgive us
     for poor judgment.
     We could push this in several directions,
                couldn't we?

Do you know what I mean?
  Policies are not repented for.
     They are explained
         defended
         rationalized
         applied
         ignored
         used to make personnel changes
            and staff adjustments
        to change the system
        to make things work out.
That means that the ones
  under the policies
        are those who have to repent
        and adjust.

That doesn't bless me a whole lot!

As anybody knows, a college chaplain's prime task is to
interpret the sanctity of the rules to the students and
to help them pray in such a way as to have a good
Christian attitude.

What other tasks a chaplain has, I'm not
really sure.

But I know he talks to people.
I live in tension because
hurting people talk to the chaplain,
people hurt by policies made by good people,
Christian people, who love God.
Christian people can apply Christian policies
in ways that destroy persons.

And we know it!

You can talk about colleges
you can talk about companies
you can talk about the church as an institution
as a body politic
they all partake of the fallenness
of the corporate structures of the world.

Now, what I have come to believe
is that in and through all this,
in a marvelous way shown for us in Romans 8:28,
(please read that wonderful verse!)
God works redeemingly
savingly
and gives us our opportunity for ministry.
Right in the midst of all this
we live and we minister.
This is the struggle we have.
And right at this point our Lord
experienced testing and struggle
as He sought to evaluate the pattern of His own
ministry.

Just think about that.
First there is the recognition of the world as is, the
status quo.
Next there is the acceptance of it,
then there is the process of working within it.
Do you see how it happens?

I got some help from a political science teacher on
campus one day when I was sharing with him the
burden of my heart about the fact that policy is never
repented for.
He said that the reason is:
policy itself is the product of compromise.
So policies are hammered and developed in compromise.
You give here to gain there.
And sometimes in the process, people are hurt.
But how can you repent for policies
that are the product of compromise?

Then, I think about the life and the ministry of Jesus
and I think of the task that we have
as we seek to fulfill the ministry He has given us.
How do we fulfill the task without compromise?
May I share some personal issues?
I have a problem
with featuring show-business people at big rallies
and highlighting them on religious TV programs
to draw crowds and enlarge the
viewing audience.
Do you know what I mean?
You see, there is among us
a fundamental desire to see the hero.
When you want a big crowd, what do you do?
Bring in some star with charisma.
That's what we do in the Evangelical church.
God have mercy on us!
We bring in a celebrity or

some politician, some fallen figure who has
been *born again* —
Someone ought to write a song: "You ain't nobody's
nothing,
'til you've been born again."
That used to be a good term.
It's a pity how it's been messed up lately.
Some popular person gets *born again*
and three weeks later we ordain him
and send him out on the road
to gather great crowds
and write books
and get rich!
And something in me says, "Oh, boo!"
He doesn't know who he is.
He doesn't know what he believes.
He doesn't understand the Christian faith.
And I think of Paul's words to Timothy:
Lay hands suddenly on no man.
(1 Tim. 5:22, KJV)
Don't be in a hurry to ordain somebody.
But isn't it a marvel how somebody
who could have been a great
famous
rich somebody for the devil
gets born again?
And all the Christians say, *Oh, isn't it just wonderful!*
So we send him out to swell the ranks.
And I wonder: To what are we catering?
What are we seeking to satisfy in
ourselves by such methods? Or is all
this just Welch's sour grapes?

Then, you know how all us Evangelicals feel about
church Bingo.
Several years ago, very close to our neighborhood,
they built a large, beautiful synagogue.

64

I think if you look at it from the top,
it looks like the star of David.
                    just beautiful.
                landscaped all around.
They had no more than finished it than they put up
a great, painted, canvas sign:
            BINGO, Wednesday night at 7:30
You could hardly see the building for this canvas sign.
                        And I thought, *Oh, no!*
                        Thank the Lord we don't do
                                        that!

We wouldn't have Bingo. It's wrong to gamble,
    but if you win the contest, you can get a bicycle.
    If your district wins, your pastor can go to the Holy
                                                Land.

        Or we'll give you a TV
            or a helicopter ride
                or at least five tickets to Disneyland.
I think about all of that.
To what does it appeal?
    It appeals to our avarice.
        I want a TV.
        I want a bicycle.
            I want to go to Disneyland.
            I want to go to the Holy Land.
    It fosters our pride and ego.
    It affirms our competitive spirit.
        Each of these we know to be marks of the carnal
                                                mind.

        Our avarice
            pride
            spirit of competition
                    are not of the Spirit,
                            but of the flesh.
And we can preach that right after making the
announcement about who's going to win the contest.

"We eat steak,
        and they eat beans,
                Praise God!"

Then, I think about the temptation of Jesus to bow
    down to Satan's sovereignty in this world.
I think about our temptation to recognize and accept
    the fallenness of our world, to work compromisingly
    within that system in order to fulfill the purposes
                    of God.
            You can see why I don't give any answers.
                    I don't know any!

And you can see why I am free to talk about this:
I haven't been a pastor since 1961.
    It's amazing how much I've learned since then.
        It's simple to explain just how churches ought to
            be holy as they work within this world!
                It's incredible how expert one becomes!
The hard part of all this
is that we *do* live in this world
    and we *do* make compromises.
        There are traditions
                and feelings
                and systems to deal with.
        There are things that happen that we do not like
            that seem to be inevitable.

But here's what I am thinking:
Aren't you glad that someone has come and lived
    among us who was not a pragmatist,
    who didn't ever compromise, and
    who did not seek to build the kingdom of God
        by capitulating to the system of the world,
            who did not do the Father's will by
                working wisely with the status quo?
I have to say,

Thank God,
the body politic is not eternal!
The chain of inevitability has been broken.
　　Into our world, fast-bound by its systems
　　　　　　　　　　and its fallenness,
　　has come One
　　　　who walked with His heart open to the Father
　　　　who paid the full price of total obedience
　　　　who never did sell out to the system.
　　　　　　　　Now that means something for me.

I know that I must live in the compromises and
　　tensions between the value structure of the Kingdom
　　　　and the value structure of the world,
but I tell you, I know what God's will is for us in this
world. Jesus has lived it out. I can bring to Him
in repentance,
　　　　the failures
　　　　the compromises of my life as I live and work
　　　　within the fallen system of the world;
　　　　　　the world He came to redeem.
This is the tension in which we live, and which can only
　　be resolved by the spirit of repentance.
I THINK THE GREAT TEMPTATION WE HAVE
　　IS TO DILUTE THE COMMANDS OF GOD
　　　　to water down the demands of the Kingdom
in such a way that we can live with them in peace.
　　While, in fact,
　　we are capitulating to the fallen systems of the world.
　　　　　　But in our humanness
　　　　　　and in our weakness,
there is open to us the way of repentance and confession
　　of openness to the God of all grace
　　whose Spirit is faithful to check
　　　　　　　　to reprove
　　　　　　　　to instruct
　　　　　　　　as we seek to find God's way in this

world.

Our faith is that the gospel is greater than the ancient
                              inveterate powers of evil.
The system is not ultimate.
God's grace is operative within it.
        It's obvious that I don't have answers to this
                                        tension.
    The problems can't be solved by saying,
            You can do this
                and you can't that.
            This is OK in the Kingdom
                but that won't do.

What the Lord is saying to me is this:
I HAVE TO KEEP THAT SYSTEM EXPOSED TO THE
JUDGMENT OF GOD AND LIVE IN A SPIRIT OF HUMILITY
AND REPENTANCE that won't let me function with
        complacency
        pride
        coldness of heart
        and self-righteousness
                while the system does its work.
At the same time, I need to be fully aware
    that the grace
    and the mercy
    and the power of God are at work
            in and through our world
                to redeem and to save.
                    Oh, I believe that, don't you?
You know, and so do I, that there have been people
    who have been hurt by good systems
        and it has turned out to be God's gracious
                                beautiful
                        providence in their lives.
                            I believe that.
            I don't see any way to be naive.
    Our institutional world is a part of the fallenness

68

of the total scheme of things.
But I can't get away from the fact
  that into the cycle of inevitability
    our pure
      honest
        obedient Lord Jesus has come
        and broken the chains.
God raised Him from the dead and laid out before us
                        His pattern
                        His life-style.

I go on living in the system
and go on attending the meetings
  that go on dealing with the problems
  that call for compromise and expediency and fiscal
                      responsibility.
What is God's will for me?
  It is to work in that system
        redeemingly
        lovingly
        sufferingly
        caringly
    willing to expose that whole system
    to God's verdict in repentance.
It is to know that in and through the whole thing
the loving
    caring
    power of God is at work.
Because, you see,
    it is precisely into the world that Jesus has come.
    God so loved the world . . .
      This world?
        With its fallenness?
        With its compromises?
        With its policies?
    God so loved the world!

Let us then with confidence draw near to the throne of grace, that we may receive mercy and find grace to help in time of need.
Heb. 4:16

5

Sharing the Victory

Well, we have been saying
that underneath the three temptation episodes,
there are two fundamental issues in the life of Jesus.
One is the temptation
to doubt the validity of His own relation to God.
The other is the temptation
to turn away from the path of suffering love and
servanthood.
I think these are ours, too.
I think, also, that the principles by which Jesus lived
are revealed in the temptation experience.
Here's what I see them to be:
First,
Jesus lived in implicit obedience to the word of His
Father.
Man shall not live by bread alone,
but by every word that proceeds
from the mouth of God. (Matt. 4:4)
Now, that was not just a verse He used to meet
temptation.
It was the word of His Father by which He lived.
It was not a tool.

It was not just a weapon.

IT WAS A WAY OF LIFE.

You know how we say in Sunday School class:
Jesus faced temptation with scripture;
so get a whole bunch of scripture
and when you have a temptation,

Thy word have I hid in mine heart . . .
(Ps. 119:11, NIV)

you can pull it out and
whack

whack your way through to victory.

No, that's dumb!

You can get a bunch of wise sayings
from Benjamin Franklin and do that.

You can, can't you?

How did Jesus use scripture?
He obeyed it!

He did *not* live by bread alone,
He *did* live by every word that proceeded
from the mouth of His Father.

For instance, in John's gospel,
Jesus keeps saying things like:

**The word which you hear is not mine
but the Father's who sent me.
(John 14:24)
I came not of my own accord, but
he sent me.
(John 8:42)
I can do nothing on my own . . . but
the will of him who sent me.
(John 5:30)
Not to do my own will, but the will
of him who sent me.
(John 6:38)
I do not seek my own glory.
(John 8:50)**

71

It is my Father who glorifies me.
(John 8:54)
My judgment is true, for it is not I
alone that judge, but I and he who
sent me.
(John 8:16)
I have given them the words which
thou gavest me.
(John 17:8)

Do you hear these words?
I don't come of my own strength,
I'm not sent of myself.
My judgment is not mine.
He lived by the word of His Father.
That's why He was able to conquer temptation.

Second,
Jesus lived with trust in His Father that asked no
proof.
You shall not tempt the Lord your
God.
(Matt. 4:7)
Jesus never did ask proof.
He trusted His Father
all the way to death.
That implicit trust opened up the way
for His Father to work in Him the marvelous miracles,
but He never demanded proof.

Then third:
He lived in a dedicated allegiance to His Father
that excluded all lesser claims.
You shall worship the Lord your God
and him only shall you serve.
(Matt. 4:10)
We are tempted
to bow down to the false system

72

and the lesser gods of this world,
aren't we?
I talked to a pastor not too long ago who said
that for 20 years, he tried to work the system and
manipulate the people within it in order to be a
success.
Now he's trying to find his own, real way.
He scarcely knows who he is.
He bowed down to the system
and became an ecclesiastical company man.
It can happen to good folks, can't it?
Well, what did Jesus say?
**You shall worship the Lord your God
and him only shall you serve.**
I hear that!

Now, here is the good word:
The victory Jesus won in His temptation
did not put Him above us as a shining example
that only reflects our tarnish.
It did not make Him the perfect pattern we cannot
follow.
Aren't you glad for that?

Rather,
THE TEMPTATIONS REVEAL THE DEPTHS TO WHICH
JESUS IDENTIFIES WITH US IN THE TIMES OF OUR TRIALS.
That means He comes and saves us from
within,
from among us.
He doesn't come from the outside,
to lift us out.
He, himself, enters into the arena of the
struggle,
and saves us from among us,
saves us from within us.
He became *one* of us,

73

He understands us.
That means everything to me.
What I am saying is that the temptations of Jesus
do not lift Him out of our arena,
  rather they bring Him into our arena
  and reveal the depths of His understanding of us.
    I see this understanding
      illustrated in the records of His dealings with
                                                people.
Do you remember the story of those who brought to
Jesus the woman taken in the act of adultery?
                    Do you remember that?
    There she was in front of our Lord,
      her accusers round about,
and Jesus, I think in embarrassment,
stooped down and wrote in the sand.
              There have been a lot of interesting
              theories about what He wrote.
Then He rose to say,
              **Let him who is without sin among you
              be the first to throw a stone at her.**
              (John 8:7)

And beginning with the oldest down to the youngest,
  one by one, they dropped their stones,
    and left Jesus alone with the woman.
Do you want to know something?
    In the presence of Jesus, all other accusers fade
                                                away.
    No earthly accuser can match that holy presence.
      That woman found herself in the presence
      of One who knew the pressure of desire
                              and appetite
                              and hunger.
    That woman was in the presence
      of One who had been lonely and empty
      with all His senses crying out for fulfillment.

74

And in Jesus' dealing with her,
He expressed His profound understanding
of the power of the senses in our lives:
Turn these stones into bread.
And He was able to say to her,
Go, and do not sin again. (John 8:11)
How can this be?
He's been there.
Do you remember when the disciples were in the ship
and Jesus came to them on the water?
Peter said,
**Lord, if it is you, bid me come
to you on the water.**
(Matt. 14:28)
Jesus understood that impulsive yearning for the
miraculous.
Didn't He?
Leap from the pinnacle of the Temple.
The angels will hold you up.
Jesus understood the hunger we have
to walk on water
to defeat the devil
to live on cloud nine
to save the world.
And He said to Peter, *come on.*
That really has helped me.
Jesus did not say what I would have said,
Peter, that's dumb. I'll be right there.
And when Peter began to fail
as he inevitably would fail,
as do we when we walk out on our waters,
Jesus was there to lift and to hold him.
He knows our hunger for miracle and magic.
He's been there!

Do you remember when Jesus was walking with the
crowds and the little man named Zacchaeus ran ahead

and climbed up in the tree to see?
Zacchaeus, the publican,
the tax collector.
We know, don't we, that a publican
is a Jew who collects taxes from Jews
to pay to Romans, and in the process
extorts from Jews
and gets rich?
No wonder he was hated and despised by his
fellows.
I see Jesus in that brief encounter with Zacchaeus
deal with him with amazing understanding and
empathy.
I believe that when Zacchaeus began his life work
as a tax man
or maybe an accountant in the local law firm
he had high visions
and lofty dreams of integrity and
honesty.
He had good intentions and good policies, but you
know how it is,
you cut a corner here,
and you make a profit there,
because a man's got to live.
So he fell into that ancient trap,
which is the devil's delusion.
You know, and so do I, that the business people in our
churches,
the lawyers
the bankers
the doctors
the teachers
the salesmen
the ministers
began their work with high dreams and hopes of
integrity

authenticity
and ministry.
But it is so easy to capitulate to the system
to quit fighting city hall
to roll with the way it is
and to capitalize on it.
Jesus knows that.
And what I see is that in His own life,
and in His relationships with us,
He's able to enter in at deep levels
to save us from within,
because He really knows us from within.
He's been there!
Do you remember Jesus' dialogue with Peter and
Peter's loud proclamation?
"I won't deny you."
"Yes, you will."
"No, I won't!"
But he did.

In full awareness of his failures, Jesus prayed for him.
He looked at Peter, restored him,
and renewed his commission.
That is every disciple's story.
In our temptations, somewhere along the
way, we have our failures.
But Jesus has suffered being tempted.
He is able to succor those who are being tempted.
He is not untouched with the feeling of our infirmity.
He was tempted in all points as we are,
yet without sin.
So what does that say to us?
**Let us therefore come boldly unto
the throne of grace, that we may
obtain mercy, and find grace to help
in time of need.**
(Heb. 4:16, KJV)

O Lord,
You have entered into our real world
         and been tempted in all points like ourselves;
    You have come to us savingly,
         to express to us, personally,
              the love of the Father for the world
                        in its fallenness.
We who live in it seek to follow You as Your disciples;
we come to You with joy this day.
    You are our God.
    You are our champion.
    You have won for us the victory that we share.
    In all the anomalies
                inequities
              weaknesses of our lives
       as we live in Your grace,
              there is strength for our weakness
              there is grace for our needs
              there is love in our lack
              there is the gracious presence of Your Spirit.
                        We do thank You!

So, in our times of stress,
    give us grace to look to You, Lord Jesus,
    and to receive from You the strength that You can
                        give us.
              For in Your name we pray,
                   Amen.